California

"The attraction and superiority of California are in its days. It has better days, and more of them, than any other country."

Ralph Waldo Emerson, *Journal*, 1871.

Travel Publications

Michelin North America
One Parkway South, Greenville SC 29615, U.S.A.
☎ 1-800-423-0485
www.michelin-travel.com
TheGreenGuide-us@us.michelin.com

Manufacture française des pneumatiques Michelin
Société en commandite par actions au capital de 2 000 000 000 de francs
Place des Carmes-Déchaux – 63 Clermont-Ferrand (France)
R.C.S. Clermont-Fd B 855 200 507

© Michelin et Cie, Propriétaires-éditeurs, 2001
Dépôt légal mars 2001 – ISBN 2-06-000131-5 – ISSN 0763-1383
Printed in France – 03-01/4.1

Typesetting : NORD COMPO, Villeneuve d'Ascq
Printing and Binding : I.M.E., Baume-les-Dames
Cover design: Carré Noir, Paris 17ᵉ arr.

THE GREEN GUIDE:
The Spirit of Discovery

*The exhilaration of new horizons,
the fun of seeing the world,
the excitement of discovery: this is
what we seek to share with you.
To help you make the most of your
travel experience, we offer first-hand
knowledge and turn a discerning eye
on places to visit.
This wealth of information gives
you the expertise to plan your own
enriching adventure. With THE
GREEN GUIDE showing you the way,
you can explore new destinations
with confidence or rediscover old
ones.
Leisure time spent with THE GREEN
GUIDE is also a time for refreshing
your spirit, enjoying yourself, and
taking advantage of our selection
of fine restaurants, hotels and other
places for relaxing.
So turn the page and open a window
on the world. Join THE GREEN
GUIDE in the spirit of discovery.*

Contents

Victorian Architecture, San Francisco

St. Helena Farmers Market, Napa Valley

Cable Car, San Francisco

© Edward Thomas

Oscar Statue (Academy Award)

© Reuters Newmedia Inc/Corbis

Maps and Plans

COMPANION PUBLICATIONS

Map 493 Western USA and Canada

Large-format map providing detailed road systems; includes driving distances, interstate rest stops, border crossings and interchanges.
– Comprehensive city and town index
– Scale: 1:2,400,000 (1 inch = approx. 38 miles)

Map 930 USA Road Map

Covers principal US road network while also presenting shaded relief detail of overall physiography of the land.
– State flags with statistical data and state tourism office telephone numbers
– Scale: 1:3,450,000

Map 933 USA Recreational

Descriptive section with color photos and profiles of 51 national parks complements a fold-out map of the US designating 500 parks, monuments, historic sites, scenic rivers and other recreational points of interest.

Historical Map of California, detail, drawn by Carolus Allard (1696)

Courtesy Bancroft Library, University of California, Berkeley

LIST OF MAPS AND PLANS

Using this guide

The guide is organized into 13 tourism regions, each with its own introduction. Each **Entry Heading** is followed by a map reference; tourist information phone number and web site (when available); and population figure (where applicable).

● Following the names of sights mentioned in this guide you will find useful information in *italics*: sight location addresses, recommended visiting times, opening hours, admission charges, telephone numbers and web addresses. Symbols used in sight, descriptions include: ⟨ wheelchair access, ⏸⏸ long lines, ✗ on-site eating facilities, ⚠ camping facilities, ⚑ on-site parking (parking indicated for points of interest in Berkeley, Los Angeles, Monterey, Oakland, San Diego and San Francisco only) and ⬛ sights of special interest to children. In Los Angeles, the ● symbol indicates the closest metro stop; in San Francisco, symbols indicate cable car ⬛, Muni ⬛⬛⬛, and BART ⬛⬛ lines that access the area.

● Many entries contain digressions, entertaining breaks from sightseeing, that are marked by a purple bar. Those digressions that appear on a map within the guide are indicated by the symbol ❶ with the number identifying it on the map.

● Sections with a blue background offer **Practical Information**, such as available transportation, entertainment, shopping, sightseeing, sports and recreational opportunities.

● The **Address Book** sections, edged with a marbleized band, throughout the guide, feature detailed information about hotels and restaurants in specific regions. Addresses, phone numbers, opening hours and prices published in this guide are accurate at press time. We welcome corrections and suggestions that may assist us in preparing the next edition. Please send your comments to:

Michelin Travel Publications
Editorial Department
P. O. Box 19001
Greenville, SC 29602-9001
Email: TheGreenGuide-us@us.michelin.com
Web site: www.michelin-travel.com.

© Edward Thomas

Legend

★★★ **Worth the trip**
★★ **Worth a detour**
★ **Interesting**

Sight Symbols

▭▷◉━━━━━▬▬▬ Recommended itineraries with departure point

⛪ ✡ ☐	Church, chapel – Synagogue		▭ ▬	Building described
○	Town described		▭ ▭	Other building
AZ B	Map co-ordinates locating sights		▪	Small building, statue
▪ ▲	Other points of interest		◎ ⚬	Fountain – Ruins
⚒ ⌒	Mine – Cave		🛈	Visitor information
🗙 ⚑	Windmill – Lighthouse		⬯ ⚓	Ship – Shipwreck
☆ ⛪	Fort – Mission		🌟 Ⅵ	Panorama – View

Other Symbols

🛡 Interstate highway (USA)	🛡 US highway	(180) Other route	
🍁 Trans-Canada highway	🛡 Canadian highway	🛡 Mexican federal highway	

Highway, bridge		Major city thoroughfare	
Toll highway, interchange		City street with median	
Divided highway		One-way street	
Major, minor route		Pedestrian Street	
15 (21) Distance in miles (kilometers)		Tunnel	
2149/655 Pass, elevation (feet/meters)		Steps – Gate	
△6288(1917) Mtn. peak, elevation (feet/meters)		△ 🏛 Drawbridge - Water tower	
✈ ✈ Airport – Airfield		🅿 ✉ Parking – Main post office	
Ferry: Cars and passengers		◻ ✚ University – Hospital	
Ferry: Passengers only		🚂 🚌 Train station – Bus station	
←←↰ Waterfall – Lock – Dam		● Ⓜ Subway station	
— ·· — ·· — International boundary		➊ ⌂ Digressions – Observatory	
— — — — State boundary, provincial boundary		▭ ▭ Cemetery – Swamp	
🍇 Winery			

Recreation

•━○○○○○• Gondola, chairlift		(⌒⌒) ⚑ Stadium – Golf course	
🚂 Tourist or steam railway		❄ ▭ ▨ Park, garden – Wooded area	
⚓ △ Harbor, lake cruise – Marina		Ⓢ Wildlife reserve	
🏄 ☑ Surfing – Windsurfing		☺ Ⅵ Wildlife/Safari park, zoo	
▨ 🚣 Diving – Kayaking		— — — — — Walking path, trail	
🎿 🎿 Ski area – Cross-country skiing		🚶 Hiking trail	
	☺ Sight of special interest for children		

Abbreviations

NP	National Park	SP	State Park	SR	State Reserve
NM	National Monument	SHP	State Historic Park	SB	State Beach

Dry lake – Intermittent river

Cable-car terminus, line □ Ghost town

🛡 🛡 National – State Park 🔺 🔺 National – State forest

All maps are oriented north, unless otherwise indicated by a directional arrow.

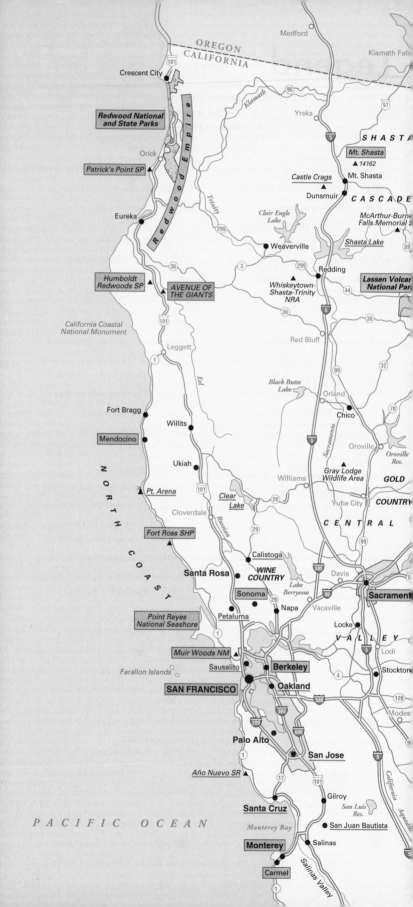

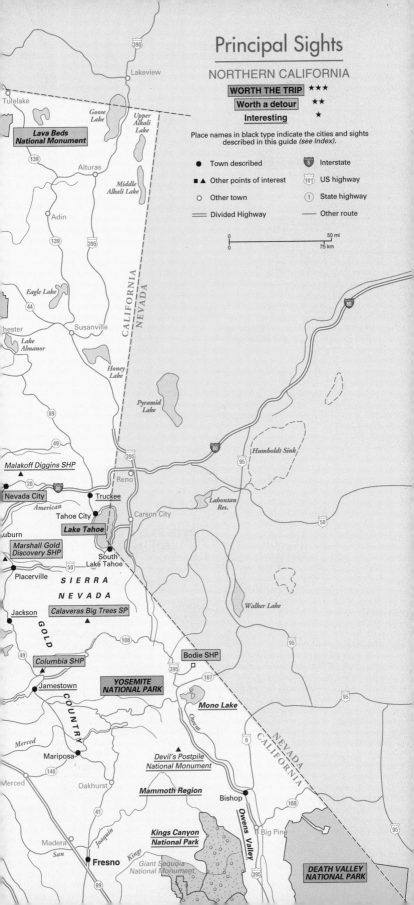

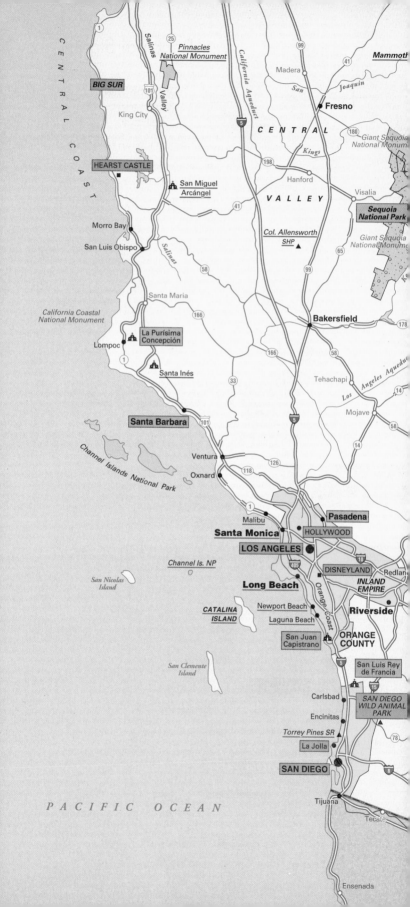

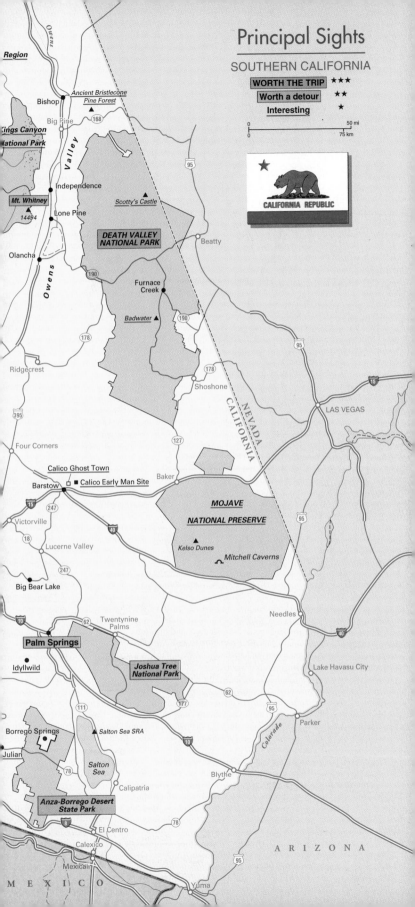

Principal Sights

SOUTHERN CALIFORNIA

WORTH THE TRIP ★★★
Worth a detour ★★
Interesting ★

0   50 mi
0   75 km

CALIFORNIA REPUBLIC

Region

Bishop

Ancient Bristlecone Pine Forest

Big Pine

168

95

Kings Canyon National Park

Independence

Scotty's Castle

Mt. Whitney
14494

Lone Pine

DEATH VALLEY NATIONAL PARK

Beatty

Olancha

190

Furnace Creek

Badwater ▲

190

178

Ridgecrest

178

Shoshone

NEVADA

CALIFORNIA

395

127

LAS VEGAS

15

Four Corners

Calico Ghost Town

Barstow   ■ Calico Early Man Site

Baker

15

247

MOJAVE

NATIONAL PRESERVE

95

Victorville

40

18

Lucerne Valley

Kelso Dunes ▲

⌒ *Mitchell Caverns*

247

Big Bear Lake

Needles

10

62

Twentynine Palms

Palm Springs

40

Idyllwild

Joshua Tree National Park

Lake Havasu City

111

177

62

95

Parker

Borrego Springs

Salton Sea SRA ▲

10

Julian

78

Salton Sea

Blythe

Calipatria

Anza-Borrego Desert State Park

8

78

El Centro

A R I Z O N A

Calexico

Mexicali

M E X I C O

95

Yuma

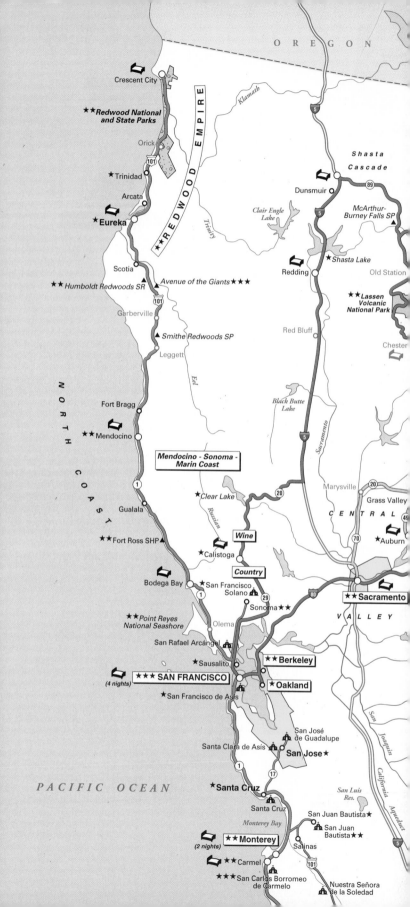

OREGON

Crescent City

★★ **Redwood National and State Parks**

Orick

101

★ Trinidad

Arcata

★ **Eureka**

Scotia

★★ **Humboldt Redwoods SR**

101

Garberville

▲ *Smithe Redwoods SP*

Leggett

Fort Bragg

★★ **Mendocino**

1

Gualala

★★ **Fort Ross SHP**

Bodega Bay

★★ *Point Reyes National Seashore*

1

REDWOOD EMPIRE

Klamath

Trinity

Avenue of the Giants ★★★

Eel

Mendocino - Sonoma - Marin Coast

★ *Clear Lake*

Russian

Wine

★ *Calistoga*

Country

San Francisco Solano

Sonoma ★★

Olema

San Rafael Arcángel

★ Sausalito

★★★ **SAN FRANCISCO**
(4 nights)

★ *San Francisco de Asis*

Santa Clara de Asis

★ **Santa Cruz**

Santa Cruz

Monterey Bay

★★ **Monterey**
(2 nights)

★★ Carmel

★★★ *San Carlos Borromeo de Carmelo*

S h a s t a

C a s c a d e

Dunsmuir

89

McArthur-Burney Falls SP

5

★ *Shasta Lake*

Redding

Old Station

★★ **Lassen Volcanic National Park**

Red Bluff

Chester

Black Butte Lake

Marysville

20

C E N T R A L

Grass Valley

49

70

★ Auburn

80

★★ **Sacramento**

29

V A L L E Y

★★ **Berkeley**

★ **Oakland**

San José de Guadalupe

San Jose ★

San Luis Res.

San Juan Bautista ★

San Juan Bautista ★★

Salinas

101

Nuestra Señora de la Soledad

San Joaquin

California Aqueduct

5

PACIFIC OCEAN

N O R T H

C O A S T

Clair Engle Lake

5

Regional Driving Tours
NORTHERN CALIFORNIA

Northern California: 1,020 miles
14 days - Round trip from San Francisco

Gold Country/Sierra Nevada: 650 miles
11 days - Sacramento to Los Angeles

Coastal California: 875 miles
22 days - San Diego to Crescent City
(additional 330 miles/3 days with side trips
to missions)

○   ○   Towns described in this guide *(see Index)*

Suggested overnight stop

★★ Monterey   City or region with local map in guide

0   50 mi
0   75 km

★★ Lava Beds National Monument

Goose Lake

Upper Alkali Lake

139

Alturas

Middle Alkali Lake

299   Adin

Eagle Lake

Lake Almanor

Honey Lake

uincy

89

Nevada City ★★

★ Truckee

American

Tahoe City

★★ LAKE TAHOE

Lahontan Res.

NEVADA

South Lake Tahoe

50   Placerville

GOLD

San Andreas

COUNTRY

49

Merced

140

★★★ YOSEMITE NATIONAL PARK

Mariposa

★ Mono Lake

Lee Vining

120

Owens

★ Mammoth Region

Bishop

395

Kings Canyon National Park

San Joaquin

Kings

Giant Sequoia National Monument

Owens Valley

Independence

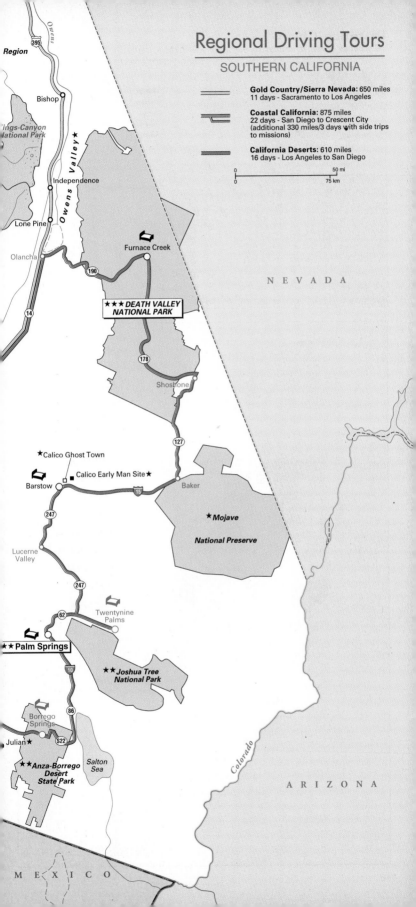

Regional Driving Tours

SOUTHERN CALIFORNIA

Gold Country/Sierra Nevada: 650 miles
11 days - Sacramento to Los Angeles

Coastal California: 875 miles
22 days - San Diego to Crescent City
(additional 330 miles/3 days with side trips
to missions)

California Deserts: 610 miles
16 days - Los Angeles to San Diego

0   50 mi
0   75 km

Region

395

Bishop

ings-Canyon
National Park

Independence

Lone Pine

Olancha

14

190

Furnace Creek

NEVADA

★★★ *DEATH VALLEY*
NATIONAL PARK

178

Shoshone

127

★Calico Ghost Town

■ Calico Early Man Site ★

Barstow

15

Baker

247

★*Mojave*

National Preserve

Lucerne
Valley

247

62

Twentynine
Palms

★★ **Palm Springs**

10

★★*Joshua Tree*
National Park

86

Borrego
Springs

Julian★   S22

★★*Anza-Borrego*
Desert
State Park

Salton
Sea

Colorado

ARIZONA

MEXICO

Distance Chart

(distances given in miles; to estimate kilometers, multiply by 1.6)

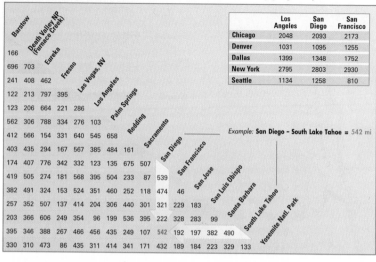

	Los Angeles	San Diego	San Francisco
Chicago	2048	2093	2173
Denver	1031	1095	1255
Dallas	1399	1348	1752
New York	2795	2803	2930
Seattle	1134	1258	810

Example: **San Diego – South Lake Tahoe** = 542 mi

	Barstow	Death Valley NP (Furnace Creek)	Eureka	Fresno	Las Vegas, NV	Los Angeles	Palm Springs	Redding	Sacramento	San Diego	San Francisco	San Jose	San Luis Obispo	Santa Barbara	South Lake Tahoe
Death Valley NP (Furnace Creek)	166														
Eureka	696	703													
Fresno	241	408	462												
Las Vegas, NV	122	213	797	395											
Los Angeles	123	206	664	221	286										
Palm Springs	562	306	788	334	276	103									
Redding	412	566	154	331	640	545	658								
Sacramento	403	435	294	167	567	385	484	161							
San Diego	174	407	776	342	332	123	135	675	507						
San Francisco	419	505	274	181	568	395	504	233	87	539					
San Jose	382	491	324	153	524	351	460	252	118	474	46				
San Luis Obispo	257	352	507	137	414	204	306	440	301	321	229	183			
Santa Barbara	203	366	606	249	354	96	199	536	395	222	328	283	99		
South Lake Tahoe	395	346	388	267	466	456	435	249	107	542	192	197	382	490	
Yosemite Natl. Park	330	310	473	86	435	311	414	341	171	432	189	184	223	329	133

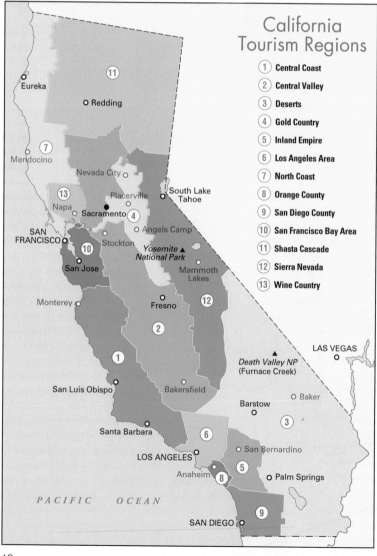

California Tourism Regions

1. **Central Coast**
2. **Central Valley**
3. **Deserts**
4. **Gold Country**
5. **Inland Empire**
6. **Los Angeles Area**
7. **North Coast**
8. **Orange County**
9. **San Diego County**
10. **San Francisco Bay Area**
11. **Shasta Cascade**
12. **Sierra Nevada**
13. **Wine Country**

THE GOLDEN WHALES OF CALIFORNIA

Yes, I have walked in California,
And the rivers there are blue and white.
Thunderclouds of grapes hang on the mountains.
Bears in the meadows pitch and fight. ...
And flowers burst like bombs in California,
Exploding on tomb and tower,
And the panther-cats chase the red rabbits,
Scatter their young blood every hour.
And the cattle on the hills in California
And the very swine in the holes
Have ears of silk and velvet
And tusks like long white poles. ...
Goshawfuls are Burbanked with the grizzly bears.
At midnight their children come clanking up the stairs.
They wriggle up the canyons, nose into the caves,
And swallow the papooses and the Indian braves.
The trees climb so high the crows are dizzy
Flying to their nests at the top.
While the jazz-birds screech, and storm the brazen beach
And the sea-darts turn flip-flop.
The solid Golden Gate soars up to Heaven.
Perfumed cataracts are hurled
From the zones of silver snow
To the ripening rye below,
To the land of the lemon and the nut
And the biggest ocean in the world.
While the native sons, like lords tremendous,
Lift up their heads with chants sublime,
And the bandstands sound the trombone, the saxophone and xylophone
And the whales roar in perfect tune and time.
And the chanting of the whales in California
I have set my heart upon.
It is sometimes a play by Belasco,
Sometimes a tale of Prester John.

Vachel Lindsay, *Collected Poems.* 1923

Morro Bay near San Luis Obispo

Marilyn Norcivestlo